Y0-AIM-731

AOTEOROA:
New Zealand Poems

by Jane Graham George

Copyright © 1999 by Jane Graham George

ISBN: 1-890193-08-9

Illustrations by Faser George

Published by:
Red Dragonfly Press
307 Oxford St. N.
Northfield, MN 55057

Acknowledgments:
"Birds of Great Barrier" appeared in *Poetry Australia*, #120, 1989.
"Historical," "For Lillie, Still Three," "Lingua Franca," "I was driving around with a plate" and "Venus de Milo" appeared in *Words Before That*, #1, 1989.
"Galloping Meditation" appeared in *Spirit Horse*, #2, Fall 1998.

**For Fraser, Lillie &
the Auckland Poetry Workshop**

Contents

Birds of Great Barrier ✸ 1
In the Awana ✸ 3
The View from Barry's ✸ 4
Venus de Milo ✸ 7
I was driving around with a plate ✸ 9
Christchurch ✸ 11
Christmas Day & ✸ 12
Southern Crossing ✸ 13
Historical ✸ 14
Lingua Franca ✸ 15
For Lillie, Still Three ✸ 17
Pohutukawa ✸ 19
Otahuhu ✸ 20
Auntie Dawn ✸ 21
Piha ✸ 23
Bluebottles ✸ 25
Haymaking ✸ 26
Immigrant's Lament ✸ 28
Gulls ✸ 29
Galloping Meditation ✸ 31

Glossary ✸ 34

Aotearoa: New Zealand poems

BIRDS OF GREAT BARRIER

If it weren't for the kingfisher
slanting in above the death's head
colour of pacific
I would stop naming

I don't remember now how long
I've lived
on this island
I might have just hatched
at night in the bare
macrocarpa limbs
with the moreporks my head
turning sharp
like theirs to follow the movement
under the ti tree
and careless
at the jets returning to L.A.
no words for any of it
just another shadow crossing the moon

daytimes I walk down slow to the river
stand brown with the cattails
lose my eyes
to the ruby-slippered pukekos
and move off
with them
into the lengthening
spaces

downriver
closer
to that broken up blue
boat always run aground
at low tide

if it weren't for the lucky fantails
the swallows in the paddock
diving every evening in the ancient
twilight and the kingfisher coming
again tomorrow always reminding past

with all the now
my own dumb feathered beauty
I could even contemplate
losing my
workmanlike fingers
to the sawn-off
hammerhead asleep forever
at noon in the Awana

Jane Graham George

IN THE AWANA

When I wake and hear the tui
subdue the blue surf
from over the hill
I begin to feel I might know
from my own unclaiming
senses walking daily to nightfall
more than any empty note above the river
more like a meteorite
of selflessness
among all my island
friends singing just
like tui in the puriri.

THE VIEW FROM BARRY'S

This land belongs
to a man from Invercargill
who wears a safari hat when he's here
and listens to a leather-covered
transistor radio the kind you can hold
in the palm of your hand
the sort to which I listened
in my back yard in St. Paul Minnesota
it was Booker T & the MGs

Here on the Barrier
you get the news
talkback radio and the races

Betting is a serious business
anywhere

Barry makes tea
and spreads the jam thin
on the crackers because going
to the store takes all day here

He stacks the manuka and shows
me how he rescues flies from
spiders without ever harming either
even so the conversation
often lags

Jane Graham George

I can easily imagine myself
at the Rialto in the
velvet seats
watching James Bond and Odd Job
in Fort Knox

Sitting in this eternal cross-
legged waiting posture and
with the 7th at Matamata
in the background the
gregorian chant
I wonder is it worth
the chance
of remarking
again on the penthouse view
when Barry already knows
how high it is here
maybe the highest place
in the Awana

The wind blows hard
through the pines he planted
as carefully
as the passionfruit
and it's the best place to be
in a storm
I can see thunderheads coming and
going almost to where I forget they
were ever right on top of me

Out to sea are
dolphins and whales some days
rock columns as changeable
as the weather as any stand of trees
as changeable and risky as my own mind
in the face of this remote island
and calm man from Invercargill

Jane Graham George

VENUS DE MILO

for Pamala Karol, "La Loca"

Once in Otahuhu
I saw a sheep driving
a truckload of humans
to the freezing works
cloud formation
through the old tyranny
still everywhere

Eat or be eaten the man was saying
and the conversation was pretty tame
we remembered to stay in lower case

Then you told him about merdevores
and I was thinking of the one who ate
200 hits of acid and had a happy reign
(the Electric Foetus on all fours)

We were dining with Ali Baba
and the 40 thieves
who kept telling us
afterwards you have to be somewhere
of course we both had a date
with the thin man
but we weren't in too big a hurry

You were rebelling with your truthful lies
as always forks and knives me and mines flying

while I prepared to eat my words
just in case they remembered the Lebanon

Tell me, did you think I
grew up in Hollywood
because I climbed upon the
altar as if I really would
give in as if I really was acting brave
when all I really planned to do was say
like the bandit of the flesh
"vamanos muchachas"

Fleece girl
you did it the best because you
got behind the cloud wheel
and ate all that shit
not scared
but just
perfectly
unarmed

Jane Graham George

I was driving around with a plate
on the dash
as if expecting
the last supper
of Assisi
to take form in my Austin.
A bristling, mustachioed
gentleman from the police
force asked me how
I had known
to expect the best chefs
of Acapulco.

Sooner or later
it all becomes clear

"When words and their meanings
are simultaneously known
in their harmonious blend
and consciousness becomes deliberately
engrossed in this new kind of knowledge.
This is known as savitarka samapatti or
thoughtful transformation.[1]

Anyway mingling the so mundane

---

[1] from *The Yoga Sutras of Patanjali*, translated by B.K.S. Iyengar

with the as yet unrevealed
proved
the best thing to say
to Officer Godbout on his rounds and wondering
about the precise make model & vintage
of my vehicle in Bel-Air.
You see I had airlifted the thing
right over the pacific via thoughts & so
clumsy still was
I
that it was a little
like flying a B-52 but
the view was atomic and the Officer was so
interested
I never even had to pay a dime
'cause all the time

I was saying like the main man
and the wheel woman
           om
           and
           shantih shantih shantih

CHRISTCHURCH

Last night I sat cross-legged on my bed
eating fish & chips. There were roses
on the cold walls and you lay across the room
from me. I didn't laugh when you read
the Dunedin headlines: PENSIONERS' SUPPER
STOLEN.
Soon we'll be apart, still hungry &
all the high country lost.

This morning we sit grey as prisoners on the
tour.
I watch our twin-image in the big bus mirror.
You pretend not to see me. I still admire
your yellow golf sweater.
It's just like you saying
make hay while the sun shines.
Our thighs just touch.

The driver's announcing Mt. Cook. In cloud.
Come on, here before all these stolid speakers
of English, these wee Scots ladies
and sturdy sheep, let's genuflect
like we did yesterday in Christchurch,
make love & history move just a little
faster than this pastureland,
cross ourselves with the dateline & meet
as sun and moon, unlikely but forever.

Christmas Day &
we're like Whitman over the continent
it's just bigger than a galaxy
ghost buffalo agallop and
I'll teach
you to ride too
below I'm exulting
home the prairie farmland
winter of old pattern
black & white and
the gray undiscovered badland
Jesse James and the most promising outlaws
hanging
out therein & here I go trancelike
in our several so long embrace
same latitude but

Thanks to all well made canoes
that traverse the worlds
the newness of it all
driving north on the southern
motorway midsummer
pohutukawas
gumboot in the left lane
Rangitoto over my right
shoulder smiling like
a greenstone

Jane Graham George

SOUTHERN CROSSING
(In Place of a Lost Photo)

I search in vain for a picture
of the happy couple, instead
remember you on deck:
the Kaikouras rise behind
like a solemn, blessing nimbus,
frame your dark hair blowing.
We're crossing the Cook Strait.
The seas pitch, chairs slide
across the galley, a free smoko
for the cook, everyone on board
but us is sick. 10 minutes before
the holy rollers warned us
against eating sweet cakes,
now they're leaning over the side.
You and I hold each other fast
hoping our dark but separate passion
lasts well past sunny Blenheim and
the train to Christchurch.
My unflinching lens takes in
the lot, unending rain and kisses,
all the way to the tame keas
and grey falls of Fiordland.

HISTORICAL

The Nurseryman warns of
these hybrids
over-refined too
lyric unhardy
but they are (blue moon and
stainless steel) so like
the age & impermanent
as greensleeves
hydroplaning out of
the Vienna woods and selling
ice cream on my block
to adults. I suppose
He would claim to prefer
a bloodrusty chrysanthemum
No matter. I push
the wheelbarrow pre-romantic
tumult with the choice two
unblooming and sing
lavender's blue
glad to escape
any kind of fascism
so feeling.

Jane Graham George

LINGUA FRANCA

1.

Chinese poet Gu Cheng wears a
distinctive greyish-green
teacosy hat

to protect his head
from words.

2.

The Armenian child
earthquake survivor
buried in rubble
hearing his father
calling repeatedly
could not cry for help
because

if he had opened his mouth
it would have filled with earth.

3.

Lillie, three, composes
sense:

Tibithy hop
the words ran out of the head
& the bones went
pop pop pop

FOR LILLIE, STILL THREE

Air raid siren.
I never know
if it's a
40s film
London under siege
      or
having learned
my letters
me crawling
under
the wooden desk &
diving through the lilacs
      looking
above the goodbye
for something past
the bombers in my sleep.

It must have been
the melon curve of your
      face,
Lillie, waiting,
still three,
never lifting your eyes
from your water colour &
waving to every plane
as if it were full of the brothers
uncles and grandfathers
who fell just like tears

from the great
           dreaming
                      horse

and now
you pick up
that tamarillo and
bite into it,
smiling like
Helen of Troy.

Anzac Day 1989

Jane Graham George

POHUTUKAWA

Cliff-dwelling pohutukawa,
   you reach out with gnarled sailors' arms
      to the Hauraki Gulf where graceful rays and sharks await
         our return, gliding soundlessly in their greenstone grave.

I tarry here with you under the bluest December skies
   stretch my limbs beneath your evergreen leaves and
      flowers like ten thousand red St. Elmo's fires,
         feel the warming earth and fathom the old tars' truth.

Like Newton, ashore, I contemplate what appears solid,
   how it moves, light theory, wave-crash, sea-smell,
      and through these thirsty senses drink it all up hearty
         in just this moment, flowering with you, bright pohutukawa.

OTAHUHU (Freezing Works)

staunch buoy in this oil-pitch night
a white dog waits mute centurion
in the jacob's ladder of light shining
from the doorway of this long campaign &
bloody sea of man's killing work

behind the sturdy dog row & row
of carcasses hang from steel hooks
curled like beckoning fingers in the wind
coming steady as the redemptive fog
off the grey-mantled Manukau

a man in once-white gumboots
red-splashed butchery gear
pockets of sawblades filet knives
skates onto the loading dock
greasy with rendering
cowflesh human toil &
stands in the light

"here, mate" he says &
casually flings a hock
to the stocky terrier who
catches it neatly
soldier-like
quick and square with death
outside man's ken

Jane Graham George

AUNTIE DAWN

for Fraser

Her people came from Rotorua
green heart of the North Island
16 year old kid she cared
for you 3 little pakeha boys
no blood tied you
only kindness
caused her to steal
from Mr. Parbhu's dairy
packaged food
easy to pocket
in her skirt
she told you you'd get a hiding
if she ever caught you doing the same

From the marae you went pighunting
with her older brothers and
the best mongrel dogs
and got a taste for puha

For this blasphemy
may her blessed ancestors
forgive me or praise me if they like
but I pass over Te Rauparaha
vanquisher of the English
and all the other chiefs of war
and I say
lay the ceremonial cloak

bright with feathers of tui
green kea and kiwi
lay it instead on Auntie Dawn
with the greatest reverence for that girl
as though you were nearing the sun itself
and ask her to raise high
the taiaha of love for all to see

Jane Graham George

PIHA

for Robert Sullivan

through the cold spray
from waves white grey & crashing
like a thousand foot soldiers
our own human shapes disappear
frivolity is dashed

here no children make castles
mine huddles in my arms
hooded dressed for winter
watching with no urge to follow
our terrier chasing the riderless
saddled horse half a mile down the coast

the setting sun is lost
behind the chill mist
where surfers sit on their boards
among the towering waves waiting

like your ancestors
out beyond the biggest surf
at the invisible horizon
in their war canoes

the wrench of their haka
reaches us as the wave crash
the seafoam encircling our feet

**we stand here quite
alone at land's end
the farthest outpost
of the known world**

Jane Graham George

BLUEBOTTLES

I tiptoe barefoot over these bluebottles
jellyfish strewn across the Awana white sand
like the sidewalk with broken glass
in L.A. where always in a moving car I see
on Vermont Street the Salvadoran
fruit seller standing proletarian grey
with his sweet oranges Sunday mornings
under the Santa Monica freeway overpass
how can he be at home I think
& blink back to this southern
hemisphere sun chiding myself
parallels are impossible when nothing
could be farther from California
than this Great Barrier Island the crashed
blue rowboat and dead hammerhead
is home then this work of finding beauty I
create no statues of Marx or Engels instead
recall the pyramid of oranges & kneel down
to the canvas before me all of the poison
india-ink pointillism shining seafoam bubbles
jewelled physics of sunlight & the freeing tide

HAYMAKING

I pause in the 4 o'clock glow
kneel to watch what we do
rock my head as drunken
as the tuis
with mown timothy
and the nectar
of late summer sun.

Mike O'Shea points to
the pink ladies dotting the hill
above the splintering barn
improbable as flamingos
these lillies grow wild
from Fitzroy to Tryphena.

Red-haired Helen O'Shea
smiles, reaches down
her broad hand, and
pulls me up to drive
the antique tractor.

The baby on my lap and I both
turn the wheel this field
might be the Indian subcontinet
you and the other men Arjuna
and his warrior knights.
God-men you swing
the bales on board

Jane Graham George

the wagon behind us.
Your arms, the dust and sweat,
this strength of men
is the purest beauty.

The Irishman scoops up
a handful of earth
breathes in its grog
and reminds me of my luck
today
when tomorrow
we shall board the scow
cross the Hauraki Gulf
dive in at noon with the makos
and one day years and
contintents away
look up through the
hardwood firmament
past the blue one beyond,
and remember this island day
and sip from it as from a chalice golden.

IMMIGRANT'S LAMENT
(waiting for a bus at 8th & Marquette)

with fierce gales
from the prairies
of saskatchewan
blowing down
the skyscraper-shadowed
city blocks of this chill
american city
i'm bound in dull mammal fur
hibernating muskrat raccoon
this too large coat
a woolen grandmother-knit scarf
coming unraveled
cloddish great boots
and i breathe cold fire
like the angry norse gods
from whom i am not descended
and to whom i feel
no connection
clad in my lava-lava
barefoot idle icarus
aesthete waiting for the sunset
on a white sand beach
near the mild equator or
somewhere down under
i might even be leaping naked
at the sight just like
my own pan hanuman or maui

Jane Graham George

GULLS

There are no happy gannet cliffs
on this land-locked prairie
where winter is a pale kind
of subterranean art.

We don't swim but toil
on the gray surface
like rock climbers
belayed to the horizontal.

Any marine sounds
are out of place,
especially in early March,
the month cast out like
an old, discolored freezer.

Yet, it's no mistake.
We both see them,
two inland gulls,
distant as planes,
their bellies silver in this season's
angle of tentative sunlight.

The high sound comes again,
kee-kee-kee, kee-kee-kee,
and breaks at our chests
like the waves at Makara,
where we climbed along

the rocky beach, stopped,
and hugged each other, just
for the warmth of it.

Impulsive now,
we unwrap our scarves,
quicken our strides,
jump iced-over early spring puddles
just as if they were the tidepools
of that subtropical land
whose bounty we shared
with gulls and sky.

Jane Graham George

GALLOPING MEDITATION

The long horizon above the pasture
where I gallop is the canvas
I have always been racing to meet
the gray alphabet of geese
in an early winter sky
draws me, a weary somnambulist,
to reach for that vast wakefulness,
love for all life, framed word,
and unrhyming art but
I fight the cold sleep & find
I must warm myself with the tangible:
up this hard dirt track today I fly on
the bay quarterhorse as in summer
past sweet corn and raspberries,
the big sound of hooves on turf
like waves at Piha
water color mares' tails
in the sky this entire vista
created and felt and known
with each animal stride.

Glossary

GLOSSARY

Anzac Day - holiday similar to Veterans Day celebrating Australia and New Zealand Army Corps (who fought at Gallipoli)

Aotearoa - Maori name for New Zealand (meaning Land of the Long White Cloud, Long Bright Land, Land of the Long-lingering Daylight, etc.)

Awana - area in the center of Great Barrier Island; white sand beach in this vicinity

cabbage tree - distinctive palm tree native to New Zealand with spike-like foliage

fantail - small sparrow-like bird thought to bring good luck

Great Barrier Island - an island in the Hauraki Gulf, off the coast of Auckland

greenstone - New Zealand jade

haka - Maori war chant

Invercargill - city on the southern coast of the South Island

Kaikouras - mountain range of the South Island

kea - mountain parrot

lava-lava - a Polynesian garment consisting of a rectangular piece of printed cotton tied loosely around the waist

macrocarpa - tree of the cypress family which grows tall and spreading

makara - beach on the West Coast near Wellington

manuka - hardwood tree

Manukau - harbor off of Auckland

marae - Maori tribal meeting-ground

Matamata - city in the North Island; means headland

Maui - a roguish demigod in Polynesian belief who helped the gods to raise the vault of heaven and caught the sun in his net and stole fire in order to give it to man

Jane Graham George

morepork - small owl with a call that sounds like its name– "morepork-morepork"

Otahuhu - suburb of Auckland, site of a freezing works (slaughterhouse)

pakeha - a Caucasian, person of European descent

Piha - Big surf beach on the East coast of the North Island; literally, ripple at the bow of a canoe

pohutukawa - very large spreading evergreen with red blossoms at Christmastime (high summer in the Southern Hemisphere)

puha - wild greens

pukeko - swamp hen, bluish-colored with distinctive red legs and feet

puriri - a tree with dense, dark, timber; New Zealand oak

Rangitoto - extinct volcano which rises from the Hauraki Gulf, a distinct Auckland landmark

taiaha - war club; hardwood weapon about five feet long with pointed tongue and narrow blade; lighter version used for a chief's staff

Te Rauparaha - 19th century Maori chief

tui - mocking-bird; a small bird with a deep bell-like song

Colophon:

This edition consists of 100 copies. A green bagasse paper was used for the covers. The text paper is 20lb mimeograph paper salvaged from the trash bin. The text face is Clarendon Light, a computerized font. The title strip was letterpress printed using ATF Craw Clarendon Book. This chapbook was printed, assembled & hand-stitched in the greeny month of June in Minnesota on the far side of the earth from New Zealand.

NORMANDALE COMMUNITY COLLEGE
LIBRARY
9700 FRANCE AVENUE SOUTH
BLOOMINGTON, MN 55431-4399